For Mary
forty three poems from
the Honicknowle Hills.

Kenny Knight
8th July 2009

The Honicknowle Book of the Dead

The
Honicknowle
Book of the Dead

KENNY KNIGHT

Shearsman Books
Exeter

First published in the United Kingdom in 2009 by
Shearsman Books Ltd
58 Velwell Road
Exeter EX4 4LD

www.shearsman.com

ISBN 978-1-84861-017-0

Cover photograph by Tony Frazer

Acknowledgements
Some of these poems previously appeared in the following magazines and
newspapers: *Evening Herald* (Plymouth), *Fire, Great Works, The Rialto, Saw,
Smiths Knoll, Tears in the Fence, Tremblestone.*

Many thanks to Tim Allen
for reviewing the manuscript prior to publication.

CONTENTS

for Angie Wickenden

LESSONS IN TEAMAKING

When I first learned to
pour tea in Honicknowle

in those dark old days
before central heating

closed down open fireplaces
and lights went out in coal mines

and chimpanzees hadn't yet
made their debuts on television

and two sugars
was the national average

and the teapot was the centre
of the known universe

and the sun was this yellow
thing that just warmed the air

and anthropology's study
of domestic history hadn't

quite reached the evolutionary
breakthrough of the tea bag

and the kettle was on
in the kitchen of

number thirty two Chatsworth Gardens
where my father after slurping

another saucer dry would ask
in a smoke-frog voice for

another cup of microcosm
while outside the universe blazed

like a hundred towns
on a sky of smooth black lino

and my father with tobacco
stained fingers would dunk biscuits

and in the process spill tiny drops
of Ceylon and India

which I would wipe with a tea towel
from the corner shop

I read the tea leaves
as if they were words

left over from a conversation
between two cups.

The Queue

The queue is an institution,
I'm in the middle of one right now,
part of the consumer snake,
slithering across the Post Office floor.

I'm here to pay my rock and roll bill.

If it wasn't for rock and roll
I'd save a fortune on American guitar bands.
If it wasn't for rock and roll and sex
and the daylight in your eyes.

The queue is an institution,
one of those cultural,
social and economic oddities,
the bus queue, the supermarket queue,
the queue in your rear view mirror.

Marriages begin in queues and sometimes end there.

The queue is more popular than religion.
The queue as symbol and organic artefact.
The queue is a sober adaptation of the conga.

The queue is a human invention,
up there with the alphabet, the wheel,
the paper clip, the safety pin,
rock and roll, contraceptives.

If it wasn't for rock and roll and sex,
and *The Honicknowle Book of the Dead*,
I'd probably convert to nostalgia,
stand on a street corner and form a queue
of people with a common past.

THE HONICKNOWLE BOOK OF THE DEAD

I'm waiting for the arrival of the past.
I'm standing outside a telephone box
on the corner of Parade and Crownhill Road.
I'm waiting for the newsagents
on my favourite street corner
to become Easterbrooks again.
Waiting for Dewhurst and Liptons
to make their long-awaited comebacks
like Dr. Who and the Daleks.

I'm standing aged ten or eleven years old,
midway between the bus shelter
and the fish and chip shop.
There's crowds of people,
packed four or five deep
on both sides of the Crownhill Road,
as the Queen Mother passes through West Park
on her way to the Tamar Bridge
with a pair of pink scissors
and a bottle of Plymouth Gin.

The patriots in the crowd are waving flags,
royalists take photographs for the mantelpiece
and someone in the crowd thinks
this is a fairy-tale
and someone in the crowd thinks
she'd like to be a princess
in a party dress of royal blue.
And I remember thinking
I'd never seen so many people
gathered together in one place,
never realised there were so many people
living in the world,
never saw so many hands, waving,
furiously waving,

on both sides of the Crownhill Road,
and the Queen Mother waves back,
doesn't even stop for fish and chips.

I'm waiting for the arrival of the past,
glancing back over my shoulder
down the badly lit tunnel of the last forty years
to the lost continent of Coronation Street
and the Crossroads Motel,
where the real life of television,
migrated into the living room.

So at age sixteen I go into exile
and walk under the bright lights of adolescence
down an infinity of Crownhill Roads
where The Royal Family will never live,
and I begin to fall in love
with the poetry of street corners
and I begin to save my paper-boy money
for Catherine wheels,
and I begin to save for Christmas.
And I don't want a bicycle,
I don't want a train set,
I want a garden shed
which I'll call Buckingham Shed,
I'll make this shed
a centre of popular entertainment,
a night club in the back garden
for nocturnal readings
from *The Honicknowle Book of the Dead.*

I'm waiting for the arrival of my knighthood,
waiting for a member of The Royal Family
to officially open Buckingham Shed,
to step inside onto bright red lino
only to discover it's really a Tardis,
decked out in bunting
from across the vast empires of time and space.

I'm waiting for the arrival of the past, waiting to win
the Nobel Prize for being your plaything, waiting for
The Honicknowle Book of the Dead to be published,
waiting for the fourteen Dalai Lamas to buy it
from the shop next door to the shop next door.

I Met My First Girlfriend at a Bus Stop on Honicknowle Green

I met my first girlfriend
at a bus stop
on Honicknowle Green.

I know it was my first girlfriend
as I'd never had a girlfriend before

and although I don't remember
the number of the bus
the colour was red
and so was my jumper.

When this relationship ended
I met my second girlfriend
at a bus stop.

This sequence continued
for the next half a dozen girlfriends
and was only broken by the first
of four girlfriends I met at a Bingo Hall.

I can even remember the number
that was called as we kissed
for the first time

and the year was nineteen
sixty eight or sixty nine.

After I'd worked romance
in bingo halls out of my system
I met further girlfriends
in cinemas, supermarkets,
funeral parlours.

Then in my mid to late twenties
I had no girlfriends at all,
even though I caught
buses regularly.

Then one night I started talking
to my next-to-be girlfriend
at a bus stop when her friend
came along and joined us.

We started going out as a threesome.

After waiting at bus stops for years
two come along at the same time.

Now with my mid life crisis
miles behind me
I'm starting to pull
at coffee mornings.

GRADE FOUR

I cried on my first day at school.
This is traditionally a child's privilege.
I didn't want to leave my mother alone
at the school gate like an unloved scarecrow.

I didn't want her to feel sad walking home
through the new born fields of tin cans,
that dead morning, when separation
was the next dish after breakfast.

I'm modest enough now to admit it,
I've still got the tears somewhere.
I take the handkerchief out now and then
like a souvenir from a weepy movie
and dab early childhood from my eyes.

Later I failed the eleven-plus
a year or so after Tim failed his,
which I regret now,
not the fact that Tim failed his
but because I could have taken the day off
and headed for Portland with my notebook.

Five years later I graduated from academia
with a grade four in Modern History.
This wasn't remarked upon in the global press at the time.
I suppose men walking on the moon was considered
more newsworthy than a schoolboy walking home
across Honicknowle Green with a C.S.E. certificate.

And the same grade in Religious Knowledge
never motivated any angels to fly over the garden,
which was mostly cabbages,
and if God ever called to offer extra tuition
no-one ever said.

My formal education ended there
soon after I left home for the streetlights
and the covens of blues and rock,
spending three or four evenings a week
at night school, learning how to spell
backwards in the bad book dark.

COMEBACK

I want my teddy bear back,
the one the dustman took away for burial
to teddy boy bear heaven.
The one who sat on the back of the lorry
looking out in dumb indifference
as Duncombe Avenue
and Little Dock Lane slipped past.

This was in the era
when Elvis Presley sang to us
teddy bear song after teddy bear song
in the days after Sam Phillips
and Presley's slow slide from integrity.

I was quite young then, and innocent.
My visible friend became invisible,
and spent the next few nights
wrapped in a newspaper shroud
on the far side of the coal shed,
a hundred yards or so as the plastic crow flies
from the box-room where I slept dreaming
of Grand-daughter Grizzly's homecoming,
like a war hero from the toy hospital
draped in an American flag
from Theodore Roosevelt's collection.

This was before I discovered
the only beds the toy hospital had
were mattresses from generations of sleep
and that no toy ever came back,
once it had crossed over Laira Bridge
into the afterlife of childhood
where sunlight reflects collectively
off cracked and broken Brylcreem jars
representing the downside
of living in a consumer society.

The rough and tumble of children at play
condemned the bear to spend eternity
wedged between a fridge and a coffee table.

At the council dump you get
a different kind of funeral director.

This was my first encounter with loss.
The teddy bear who never came back,
who may or may not have died in a toy hospital
in a bed next to a hippopotamus or circus clown.
Sadly I believe the latter to be untrue,
although I prefer the image of inanimate objects
on the brink of breath.

I waited until the sunset after next
before I fell asleep in the arms of a giraffe,
or was it a donkey on wheels?
I can't remember all the toys I went to bed with.
I was so promiscuous.
Was it a giraffe or was it a cuddly raven?
Two big black arms in the sky of my sleep.

Grand-daughter Grizzly went missing in the summer holidays,
shortly after my discovery of a frog, crossing the backyard
one morning, on its way to breed in Ernesettle Creek.

I wanted to keep the frog in a bucket of water
inside Buckingham Shed Zoo.
My father helped it escape this prison
by promising it would return that autumn
from its marriage bed of mud.

This was my second encounter with loss.

The frog moved into the shadows
of the cabbage patch,

distancing itself from my father's little green lie.
I thought about the frog until September
brought October and distraction.

Maybe it returned and maybe
it moved from pond to pond
splashing its seed around
avoiding small boisterous boys
who played centre forward
in the mud and rain of the football season.

Maybe it passed through in the dead of night,
attracting moths with its bright eyes and sticky tongue.

Maybe it ran off with Grand-daughter Grizzly
and taught her to catch dragonflies.
Maybe they cohabited down on the creek,
moving into a hut of mud
to spawn future generations of amphibious bears.

HUMMINGBIRD

Miss Paris tried to make me eat thick custard
in the dinner hut in primary school.
I never liked thick custard or blancmange
and I wasn't too keen on Miss Paris either.
Miss Paris surely had better things to do with her time,
like paint fingernails the colour of a red Hummingbird.
Loud as fuck she'd play 'Telstar' for the dinner ladies
tuning up to twang for her Teddy Boy boyfriend
who could jive better than a grizzly
who didn't look anything like Eddie Cochran
who drove a Ford Zodiac or Ford Constellation
who dipped his head in Brylcreem or lard when desperate
who was a rebel with a bad cough
who wore drainpipe trousers; when it rained
his mum pegged them to the washing line.

Miss Paris could play that Hummingbird better than
any of the dinner ladies.
This was better than custard or the wireless
which was mostly Mantovani and *Sing Something Simple.*
This was Post World War One meets Post World War Two.
This was a generation gap wider than left and right.
This was before we tuned into Radio Luxembourg,
a country small enough to squeeze
beneath the blanket or pillow.
This was before we tuned in, turned on and dropped out
with Timothy Leary, or thought we did.
This was before The Shangrilas
before Johnny Kidd and the Pirates
before the first air-guitarist emerged from the shadows to sign
a record contract for 'Four Minutes and Thirty Three Seconds',
before memory shuffled it all around the jukebox.

Miss Paris, hummingbird eyes fluttering
on Little Dock Lane, was a footnote

in the collected works of the Twentieth Century,
a hundred years thick.
Her after school dinner speeches
were pharmaceuticals for the ear.

BACK IN THE DAYS OF POUNDS SHILLINGS AND PENCE

The Queen's favourite band is
The Buckingham Shed Collective.

The Buckingham Shed Collective once played
Fanfare for the Common Man on Gardeners' World.

The Buckingham Shed Collective
gatecrashed the Eurovision Song Contest
back in the days of pounds shillings and pence.

My mum's favourite band was Ted Heath and his Orchestra.

Ted Heath and his Orchestra
never entered the Eurovision Song Contest
though they sounded nothing like Abba
when they played Waterloo Sunset.

The Eurovision Song Contest
is the main reason Britain joined the Common Market.
When The Common Market turned into The European Union,
the drummer in The Buckingham Shed Collective
became a shop steward in the House Of Commons.

My mother brought me and my two sisters into the world,
but Ted Heath took us into Europe.

Back in the days of the big band
you were either a member of The Royal Family,
a member of the nuclear family,
The Buckingham Shed Collective
or Ted Heath and his Orchestra.

Back in the days of the big bang,
one half of me wanted to be a member of Ban The Bomb,

and the other half wanted to split
the atom with my mother's nutcrackers.

Back when The Queen made her first Royal visit
to Buckingham Shed,
I wanted to rule the world
when Harry Secombe had had enough.

The first Buckingham Shed Collective tribute band
were called The Shedheads.

Back when Ted Heath orchestrated Britain's move into Europe.
the drummer in The Buckingham Shed Collective
became a member of The House Of Lords.

Back when the big band era was in its prime,
twenty to thirty big swingers stood on the runway
at Twinwood Airport to wave Glenn Miller goodbye.

The big bang gave birth to the big band.
The big bang gave birth to one of my favourite
blues rock bands
Big Brother and the Holding Company.
The big bang gave birth to democracy,
feedback, distortion,
and Ted Heath and his Orchestra.

Ted Heath and his Orchestra always voted Conservative;

when the big band era ended
Ted Heath became Prime Minister.

SKINNY

When I die bury me in Woodland Wood
underneath that tree
where we once undressed
in the dirt of multiple autumn.

Or dangle me discreetly in chains
from Blackie Bridge
where I'll conduct the river into song:
the dead waving to the living
through the medium of Ernesettle Creek
every time the train rumbles on its way
to Calstock, or back.

Inter me in the dungeons down in Knowle Fort
which I thought at an early age was a castle
where the Knights of the Round Table slept.

This was before the middle ages
and the middle classes were invented,

before the coffee table
entered the charts of popular culture
on the left wing of Tony Benn's living room.

Or lay me underneath my favourite street corner
on the Crownhill Road at West Park,
where I hung around for a year or two
somewhere between paper boy and puberty.

When I die I'll apply for housing
in The Happy Humping Grounds
and dream of our reunion in a double bed.

If I get as far as the afterlife
I'll try to get it twinned with Honicknowle,

but knowing my luck I'll get reincarnated
long before I cross over the border into St. Budeaux.

And nine months later I'll make a comeback
in the lands of the dead,
in a little cul-de-sac somewhere south of Woolaton Grove,
where the orchards grow
and the nightingales raise their families.

I know what I want to be when I grow up.
I want to be six foot two and skinny.

BACKGROUND

My background is a garden
of potatoes and cabbages.
It was popular with caterpillars.
Ants lived in the basement of the soil.
The sun was a frequent visitor,
we shared it with lots of other countries
on the planet through a rota system.
If it was night over Chatsworth Gardens
it was safe to assume the sun was shining
in some far-off corner of the long shadow
from Buckingham Shed.
Rain was considered international by the garden
which welcomed it, whatever language it spoke.

You didn't need a weatherman to tell you
Bob Dylan was on the radio or an astrologer
to predict when your birthday was.

Some of the people who lived in my street
worked at Berketex or Rank Bush Murphy
which later became Toshiba.
My father was a docker.
My mother was a housewife.
I was a media correspondent
watching the sun rise and set
slower than a newsflash.
I delivered morning and evening papers
to houses along Sherford Crescent
and Coombe Park Lane.
Night after night I'd think about being famous
like someone on the wireless or the television.
I played rock and roll on an old tennis racket
and formed my first band
with four imaginary friends
we called ourselves George London and the Capitals.

My eldest sister worked for Farleys and smelt of rusks
and fancied Billy J. Kramer and Del Shannon.

When I was a teenager I had a crush on Kathy Kirby.

I grew up in the working-class
neighbourhood of Honicknowle.
The folks who lived in my street
called the area West Park,
probably because of some inverted sense
of poshness in West Park's name.
I could never figure out where one area
was supposed to end and the other begin.
There wasn't a checkpoint
or sign saying 'Welcome to Honicknowle,
home of the lands of the dead,
twinned with the afterlife'.
'Or you are now leaving West Park,
gateway to the Blue Monkey
and the St. Budeaux Triangle'.

The highlight of any weekday
or weekend evening was to see
who got off the number twelve
or thirteen bus from town,
which was some exotic place
where grown-ups went to drink beer,
stagger on and off the bus, or fall over.

Some came home with the imported
bright lights of Hollywood in their eyes
after watching a bunch of cowboys
shoot it out under the sunset
in The Drake, The Gaumont, The Belgrave,
The Flea Pit, The Plaza, The Odeon,
Ford Palladium, ABC or Abercrombie Roadhouse,
before heading back to the dusty streets of hometown.

On both sides of the Crownhill Road
they'd strut and smoke one last cigarette
before Ovaltine and oblivion.

When I was growing up
Honicknowle had a rough reputation
exaggerated out of all proportion
like most urban myths
from the reality that existed
on its far-flung street corners.

The name West Park came from West Park Farm
which died in a hail of bulldozers.

Honicknowle is over a thousand years old
and was listed in *The Domesday Book*,
but the omission of Buckingham Shed
is a mystery Maigret thinks may be deeper
than the shallow end of Tinside Pool.

Buckingham Shed is the home of Queen Log
and her insomniac boyfriend,
who holds the World Record
for sleepwalking the hundred metres
in four minutes and thirty three seconds,
while humming the National Anthem
in the backyard to a receptive audience
of potatoes and cabbages.

In the park beyond the garden popular with caterpillars
stands a living totem, indigenous to my past,
a hermit tree in the middle of the park,
a refuge for generations of small birds
inhabiting the leftovers of the countryside.

The last time I walked through the park,
the hermit tree was in full leaf.
too far away to hear birdsong.

I wonder if the kids who live there now
listen to Radio Luxembourg under their pillows.

I remember falling asleep to rock and roll
and waking up to white noise on a battery
as flat as my backing box-room vocals.

The box-room where I first read *The Third Eye*
an autobiographical fiction by Cyril Henry Hoskins,
a plumber who reinvented himself as Lobsang Rampa,
who attained Nirvana on a pilgrimage
to Tibet and the St. Budeaux Triangle,
who reappeared on the top deck of a red thirteen,
heading east towards Chaddlewood,
with a free range chicken, a roll of carpet,
and a free range egg.

You can now catch a bus
from Honicknowle to the Himalayas
and before you've travelled halfway
become homesick for sunset
over The Blue Monkey.

If you're sensitive or psychic or have
a good ear for the death throes
of the past you can hear
the bulldozers moving in
to deliver their collective
sick note at the demolition
to Honicknowle primary
and secondary schools
and the homes that fell
on the edge of Woodland Wood.

There's no place like Honicknowle
and West Park ain't South Park,
that's for sure.

Mod

I once rode pillion on a Lambretta or Vespa
all the way down Duncombe Avenue
to the roundabout on Little Dock Lane
and all the way back up the Avenue
to Chatsworth Gardens.
Paul Giles (who was driving)
had just become a mod.
He wore a full length parka
the same shade of green as boiled cabbage.
It was the summer of Nineteen Sixty Four.
It was the year a mod from Harewood Crescent
entered the *Guinness Book of Records*
for having more wing mirrors on his scooter
than our street had cars.
I was thinking about this
after hearing a convoy of scooters
pass through the city late at night
like pilgrims from Margate and Brighton.

And I was thinking that if someone
as young now as Paul Giles was then
were to drive a Lambretta or Vespa
all the way down Duncombe Avenue
to the roundabout on Little Dock Lane
(the roundabout that is no longer there)
and all the way back up the Avenue
to Chatsworth Gardens
would he consider himself to be a mod
or post-mod
and would he be a linguist and be fluent in Italian,
as fluent as I was that day in Nineteen Sixty Four
when I climbed off the back of that Lambretta or Vespa
and looked into a dozen wing mirrors
and saw the many faces of me
and realised I had the wrong kind of hairstyle
to be a mod.

I Don't Know Much About Cars

I was born in the lands of the Land Rover
and the Tesco Metro.

I was a getaway driver in the badlands
of the swinging cities.

I named my cat after a fire engine
and my teddy bear after a police car.

I once drove a Hillman Imp or Minx
through the hills and back roads
of Mannamead and Peverell.

Then I saw the traffic light
and became a chic pedestrian,
while car drivers wore fan belts
to keep their trousers up.

When Adam and Eve left Eden
they drove off in a Vauxhall Cavalier,
and when they pulled into Lover's Lane
they parked in the lay-by
and spent the next thirty minutes
exploring glove compartments,
adjusting wing mirrors,
the loss of innocence.

The tree of knowledge
crept into the conversation
and crept out again
when they realised
it knew fuck-all
about hub caps.

I used to be a boy racer.
Recently I've been feeling nostalgic
for the golden age of the Ford Concertina.

When my dad bought his Ford Zodiac
the moon was on the cusp
of the Americans landing on it.

My wife once drove an Austin Texas,
through Austin Texas.

I've never had sex in a car,
though I once made love
to a Conservative Councillor
on a bathroom floor.

The Ford Palladium was a cinema,
my father took me to see
a Davy Crockett film there.
If the Ford Palladium had been a car
they would have made one
for each of The Tiller Girls.

LORRY

Say hello to the lorry that looks like the one
grandad gave me for my birthday
that's big and yellow and scratched
like a grown-up version of my toy.

The shoes of my lorry are muddy,
when I get home I'll drive it
down amongst the cabbages
and load it with white butterflies;
crates and crates of them,
flying inside the dark:
flakes of sentient snow.

Later I'll drive it through the streets
to the Brittany ferry
as the sun goes down like a sleeping man.
Then I'll turn my headlights towards the sea
and the butterflies loose
before driving slowly
home to my garage in the hills.

Scorpio

I was allocated one of those star signs
but didn't find out about it for twenty years.
A midwife wrapped my umbilical cord
around the constellation of Scorpio,
where spaceships revved up for some
intergalactic Grand Prix,
where some otherworldly
Murray Walker still commentates
at the speed of dark glasses.

I pulled into pit stop Plymouth,
recycled molecules eager for knitting.
Apparently the moon was in Sagittarius
although my mother swore
she saw it that night through
the maternity ward window,
while Venus waiting on
the far side of adolescence,
wore a costume that stripped
my vocal cords of sound.

I could have had my astrological chart read
if my mother had worn a wristwatch,
school of fifty one, ten days old
and still not fluent in English.

Born under a street sign,
eight houses down the road
from the No Place Inn.

The first Zodiac I knew
was Steve in *Fireball XL5*.
I was happy to leave
the constellations to Dan Dare
and Patrick Moore's telescope.

I was having fun
splashing in puddles
and rolling in mud,
too busy to think
about Scorpions or Crabs.

At night with school-friends
I'd walk through the grounds
of Higher St. Budeaux Parish Church,
daredevils twitching in the dark
above an acre or two of bone,
the creak of trees,
and tombstones leaning
like politicians to left and right.

Back in those days the backyard
was the centre of town,
and the girl next door
lived two hundred and fifty
miles away in Hatfield.

Back in the golden-oldie ghost town of the past
I was plugged into the street corner,
I started an imaginary pop band
called The Pop Pickers.

I wrote song titles that reached number one
on the Honicknowle charts.

My bedroom wall was covered with photographs
of the number twelve bus passing through Taurus
on the road to Camel's Head.

I had a crush on a blonde
film star called Doris Day,
which in later years
transferred to a brunette ball of fun

crowned Queen Log in Woodland Wood.
Woodland Wood where I roamed as a teenager,
wearing daydreams on the sleeve
of my ripped shirt;
daydreams that came and went
like weddings going nowhere
but daydreams weren't communal
like the street corner
or the moon in Pisces.

My dad drove a Ford Zodiac
around the block every night after tea.
I've no idea what star sign
my dad's Ford Zodiac was.

And now forty years after being allocated
one of those star signs
I'm looking for a lover
from the constellation of Pisces
but can't afford the airfare.

This body I wear has grown tall.
I want someone dark and compatible;
I'll cross her palm with stardust
and lose my innocence in uncut grass,
press my belly button and ejaculate into space.

I was born with the Moon
in Honicknowle,
the Sun in Woodland Wood,
Mercury in the West Park Post Office,
Mars in The Blue Monkey,
Scorpio in Buckingham Shed.

Born on the cusp of one minute to the next
in the Chinese year of the rabbit,
I'm interested in sex sex and sex,
but not necessarily in that order.

I need five things to live on this planet.
Earth, Air, Fire, Water and Money.

I play the fruit and veg machines
down at the One Armed Angel.

When Jupiter is in conjunction with Mars
and the Earth is passing through
the constellation of disorganised religion,
then I pray for a jackpot of jackdaws.

I don't care anymore
about anything to do with Aquarius.
If there ever was a golden age
it must have been full of Ford Zodiacs,
boom and bust towns
and buses loaded with miners
bringing shovels home from work.
People on stage wearing wigs in musicals
in the days of Flower Power and Free Love,
or a woman like you who never quite found
the exit from the Swinging Sixties
who thinks I'm Bruce Dern.

HAVEN

Street long as legs that walk it.
Street that breathes the past
into consciousness and lungs.

I cannot relinquish
total attachment
to tenancy.

In sleep I locate the key,
there's a number thirty two
on the door,

like an old friend
I wake in the heart of it.

Inside, peace and security
wraps a medley
of hot water bottle blankets
around my soul.

Golden light fuels every vein.

This is where the ghosts
of my family live.

This haven

from the fog

of being tall.

LAUDANUM

I'm a time traveller from the distant future
humming a Gerry Rafferty song
in the ballroom of Buckingham Shed.
I'm returning to the gooseberry bushes
at the top end of King's Road,
which every summer we raided
and plucked clean, until the day
a policewoman drove by.
I remember holding my breath
like a guilty mouse
caught drilling a hole
in Superman's Cheddar
or freeloading the stash
of Sherlock Holmes
and I'm back there now, caught
in the spotlight of memory.

And I want to travel further back in time
to when Big Ben was young
and not yet a *News At Ten* regular,
to meet the man who invented
the archetypal upper class supersleuth,
who may or may not have drank with Darwin
and Blackmore in the Blue Monkey.

And I'm waiting
to be frogmarched up Jubilee Road,
to be held tightly in a long blue arm,
waiting to step off the kerb into a police car
with the same long scarf reach
as Doctor Who's Tardis,
waiting to pull out into morning traffic
and be taken back in time custody
on a roundabout of days and nights
to the Durnford detective agency of Conan Doyle

where I'll drink laudanum and eat gooseberries
and take poetry performance enhancing drugs.

A hundred and twenty five years is a long way
to travel on a social call,
so the police car pulls itself over
and stops outside a house
on the corner of a street in Little Tibet,
the birthplace of Cyril Henry Hoskins,
the wildlife photographer,
who became Lobsang Rampa
and wrote *The Third Eye*,
Doctor From Lhasa,
The Hermit
and *The Thirteenth Candle*
after taking a photograph of an owl
while falling from a tree.

Born on the eve of the First World War
the Lama of Plympton St. Maurice
spent his childhood
in the shadow of Dartmoor.
Was he a time traveller, influenced by
The Honicknowle Book of the Dead?

When he died in Nineteen Eighty One
was he reincarnated in West Park
or the St. Budeaux Triangle?
where the streetlights glow like butter lamps
and the prayer flags migrate with the swallows
at the end of summer.

I'm a time traveller,
staying overnight in a safe house
in the People's Republic of Whitleigh,
a time traveller, walking through Woodland Wood
towards a rendezvous with Abercrombie
outside an Anderson shelter on Tamar Way.

Abercrombie is waiting to be taken
on a guided tour of Buckingham Shed
and I'm waiting in both, the past tense
and the presence of the future
to meet the man
who designed the school
where I flunked Architecture,
waiting to see the first drafts
of classrooms and corridors,
the playground, the library, the bicycle shed
and the Quadrangle where tiny lizards
hung around on the walls
waiting to be discovered
by David Attenborough.

I imagine the council houses
of Ernesettle and Honicknowle,
waiting patiently inside the pencil
Abercrombie holds in his hand;
the pencil pointing to a haven
of parks and gardens,
a place for childhood to shelter
from sun and rain.

I'm a time traveller,
consumed by curiosity,
waiting to blink and breath
and peep down the long tunnel
of the past
where the light at the end of it
is The Second World War.

On the edge of my audible range
I hear air raid sirens set to panic tone
and see bombs fall through
scream filled seagull skies
onto the rooftops of Royal Parade
and the quiet sleep of houses.

I'm a time traveller,
waiting to see the surrealist poet
Louis Aragon
as he comes ashore at Mount Wise
and stands quietly in the shadows
gazing across Stonehouse Creek,
back through ten thousand sunsets
of darkness.

I'm a time traveller
travelling back through the history of this city.
The Depression and the General Strike,
the Roaring Twenties and the First World War.
Waiting to see Scott set sail for Southampton
before sailing for the Antarctic.

I'm a time traveller,
travelling a hundred and fifty years
from the pocket watch factory of the future,
fifty years too late to see Darwin
set sail on The Beagle
from the golden sands of Devil's Point
passing Drake's Island and the Mewstone
at the start of an epic voyage of discovery
to the Galapagos Islands.

On his return in Eighteen Thirty Eight
Darwin began work on *The Origin of Species*
which the voice text on my landline
tells me was published in Eighteen Fifty Nine
as *The Origin of Spices*.

I'm a time traveller,
waiting to touch down
in a car free world,
waiting to be busted in possession
of the fiction,

waiting to see Conan Doyle
in tweeds and deerstalker,
boarding the ferry for Mount Edgcumbe.

I'm a time traveller,
a hobo of film and book,
drinking one last glass of
Doc Holliday's favourite tipple.

A police constable passes by
on a Penny Farthing,
time siren wailing
like the song of a ghost.

I'm night shopping on Millbay Road
for a bouquet of Victoria's kerbside poppies.

I'm ahead of my time by a millionth of a second,
ahead of the long time travelling arm of the law.

THE LEFT EYE OF MAE WEST

I want to browse through the junk shop of history.
I want to be smuggled into your bedroom
inside a wooden horse called Troy Tempest.
I want to think. I don't want to think.
I want to compromise with myself
over unimportant issues.

I want to sing in the bathtub with Suzanne Vega.
I want to copulate with a money machine.
I want it to come a million times.

I want to speak every language in the world
at least once in my life.

I want to walk barefoot
across the front page of your heart.

I want to discover the north-west passage
to Ernesettle Creek and be the last person
in the world to walk across the old Whitleigh Bridge
before they knock it down and rebuild it again
with bricks left over from the demolition
of Honicknowle Secondary.

I want to explore the street
where Scott was born
before it becomes an iceberg.

I want to follow the footpath that skirts Woodland Wood
as if it were a suspect in a Maigret movie.

I want to be an icon for sixteen minutes.

I want to discover the whereabouts of Miss Josephine Ebert
who is probably alive and well and living in Whitleigh.

I want to fall in love with Miss Honicknowle.

I want to be popular with groupies and hecklers
and not be able to tell the difference in bed.

I want Angie Wickenden to take me home tonight.
I want to be a toy boy before it's too late.

I want to get divorced from my wife after breakfast
and marry her again before lunch,
then go away on honeymoon just as night falls
from an open window into the arms of streetlight.

I want to buy an empty notebook and fill it with words
until it resembles an overcrowded city.

I want to be a poetry pin-up
in a small corner.
I want to write the sequel to
The Honicknowle Book of the Dead
on a notepad purchased with an Arts Council bursary.

I want to be a pirate and cut up language like Steve Spence.
I want to be a Viking in an Anne Born poem.
I want to be published in *The Rialto*.

I want to boast about it at The Language Club.

I want to be a Guest Poet just like Harry.

I want to win the Nobel Prize for Literature
in a penalty shoot-out, in a second-hand bookshop,
with the collected works of Pablo Neruda, Czesław Miłosz
and Octavio Paz, collected together as goalposts.

I want to score the winner on the last line.

I want to be an all night taxi driver
and drive around all night looking for Christmas.

I want to paint the ghost of Picasso.

I want to be a legend and eat lunch with myself.

I want to play drums in a Buckingham Shed Collective
tribute band.

I want to take James Turner's humour
out to the edges of stage-fright.

You can forget about Aleister Crowley,
I want to be an icon like Norman Jope.

I want God and the Devil to shake hands
and smile for the camera. I want to sell
the photograph to the *Daily Star*.

I want to walk hand in hand down the aisle
of some department store with the last bride
of consumerism.

I want to walk with Salvador Dalí
as he walks through Hollywood
with the left eye of Mae West in his hand.
I want to run my fingers through Mae West's hair
while it is still wet with the first blonde coat of intimacy.

Ruth Padel and the Dalai Lama

I had a dream the other night
that Ruth Padel was living in Honicknowle;
Cobbett Road, number twenty six.

I imagine Ruth Padel reading
The Honicknowle Book of the Dead
to the Dalai Lama.

I had this dream about Ruth Padel
and the Dalai Lama,
two nights before I read
at The Language Club
with Steve Spence and James Turner.

The Dalai Lama was staying
at a Buddhist bed and breakfast
centre on Chaucer Way,
from where he sent postcards
three times a week
to the rooftops of his homeland.

The postcards show Ruth Padel
walking in various locations
through the literary quarter
of Honicknowle:

Tennyson Gardens.

Byron Avenue.

Dickens Road.

In her shoulder bag
Ruth Padel was carrying
the collected works of Geraldine Monk.

There was much speculation
about the purpose of the Dalai Lama's visit.
One was to check out Honicknowle's suitability
as the venue for the first
wonder of the world
of his next childhood.
The second was a pilgrimage to
The Honicknowle Book of the Dead's
birthplace: Chatsworth Gardens.

The reason for Ruth Padel's presence
in Honicknowle is unknown, though
one possibility could be its easy access
to the tourist attractions of Woodland Wood,
Whitleigh Bridge, Ernesettle Creek
and Buckingham Shed,
which does a really nice bed and breakfast.

THE COLD WAR

The Cold War was for boys
who'd grown too big for snowballs.

The Cold War started somewhere
between Novorossiisk Road
and Little America.

The Cold War was chilly.
Propaganda was an exercise
in temperature control.

The Cold War was popular
with rocket scientists and teenagers
gathered around bonfires.

The Cold War was a series
of international incidents.

I studied espionage
and extra sensory perception
in Greenland with Greenpeace
and The Honicknowle Blues Band,
hummed colour co-ordinated songs
like 'Pink Cadillac' and 'Big Yellow Taxi'.

The Cold War's radioactive fingers
on my blue collar.

I was born in the political
climate of hypothermia.
I remember looking through
the bullet holes
of Yevtushenko's words.

Take me back to the Cold War
and Napoleon Solo.

I'd like to turn the Cold War
into a Johnny Winter blues movie.

During the Cold War
everyone in the West Park area
of the Western World
boogied to
The Buckingham Shed Collective.
In the Kremlin the iron curtains
twitched between each song.

I had a crush on Miss Moneypenny.
I signed the Official Secrets Act
on Valentines Day.

During the Cuban Missile Crisis
we played the last rites
of World War Three
in the corridors
of the secondary school
and the waters of Camel's Head Creek.

Che Guevara was a pin-up
in the bedsit revolution.

Brezhnev was a Beatles fan.
In the nightclubs of Moscow
he led the communist community singing
to the chorus of 'Yellow Submarine'
and 'Octopus's Garden in the Shade'.

The best part of the Cold War
was Ski Sunday.

Bing Crosby was my mum's favourite
Cold War crooner.

The estate agent
who looked like James Bond
took photographs of houses
in Mannamead
with a cigarette lighter.

There's more to the Cold War
than Checkpoint Charlie
and 'Back in the USSR'.

In Nineteen Eighty Two,
Queen Log spent two weeks
at Greenham Common,
sleeping on the barbed
shoulder of America.

I was inches from the television screen
when the wall came down.

If the Cold War was the dawn of
the Age of Aquarius
tomorrow should be hot.

What the World Needs Now

What the world needs now
is a bigger fridge to help
reintroduce icebergs
back into the wild.

What the world needs now
is to sing from the same bed sheet.

What the world needs now
is a Royal Box
inside the ballroom
of Buckingham Shed.

What the world needs now
is a blind date
and a bag of sugar.

Look at this wonderful
washing machine world
we all live in with its
biodegradable sunshine.

What the world needs now
is to move to Massachusetts.

What the world needs now
is a new Burt Bacharach song.

What the world needs now is
The Honicknowle Book of the Dead.

The world is held together by street signs;
learn to read and you won't be lost.

FURZEACRES

For Philip Kuhn and Rosemary Musgrave

At the start of the sunday lunchtime
long-poem reading series,
you wouldn't have found me loitering,
anywhere in the neighbourhood
of a plate of middle-class cheese,
but now, standing in the kitchen
of another Furzeacres gathering,
furtively feeding my taste buds,
unnoticed until, humming
'A Whiter Shade of Pale'
underneath his breath,
Mister Kuhn notes my defection
and whispers in my left ear:
'This is your eleventh visit
and you've sold out already'.

Crossing over from the working-class cheese quarter,
this is my first visit to first class.
I'm strictly street corner.
My mother would be proud.
I'm trying to keep my feet on the lino.
I'm a class frog leaping up the social ladder
gate-crashing the middle-class cheese and poetry crowd.

At Furzeacres the cheeses are cosmopolitan
and the poems as long as Ludgate Drive,
which is in serious need of some urban redevelopment.

Once you've tasted the heady delights of middle-class cheese
there's no going back to the dartboard.
It's time to fold up the dungarees
and smuggle them down to the charity shop,
and pick up an Ezra Pound *Collected*;

a Picasso for a song,
preferably Procul Harum.

You're unlikely to find Pound in a Pound Shop.
You're unlikely to spot the ghost of Picasso
eating cubes of cheddar in The Bagatelle.

It's a big leap from working class to middle class
but the cheese frog is working his way across the pond.

When I consider my humble roots
I feel grateful to be welcomed
into the homes of middle-class people
and invited to partake of their cheeses.

The class frogs have come from the puddles
to this bungalow on the edge of the moor,
to this sunday afternoon school of poetry
where Dairy Lea rubs shoulders with Dolcelatte.

TREEHOUSE

I wanted to go home.
I cried and I don't know why.
I was lost and the big city was famous,
too famous to know about me.

I was scared by all the legs.
It was like walking through a thick forest
walking on the pavement.
The forest was big and I was small
and far too slow to dodge
the trouserbark skirtbark trunks.

The trees didn't have roots, just shoes
although mostly not muddy.
There were even starlings and other birds
tapping their beaks on the ground.
I'd stop and listen to their songs.

It's easy to forget that collected together
people become a forest.
It's easy to forget, once you've grown
and become a tree, that you're just another part
of the moving landscape of big forest
to someone small.

Sometimes I'd imagine these trees;
pin-striped and other varieties,
dancing together to music they heard on the radio,
dancing like real trees dance to the lazy rhythms
of thundercane and tornadosong.

I liked the weather when it was raining, even then.

I wanted to explore the world but was restricted
to the margins. I was too young to be trusted
with an atlas. I always lost gloves.

I wanted to fall in love and bruise my legs.
Buttercups and dandelions hated me.

I spent half of my childhood laughing at televisions
and the other half staring, through windows
from claustrophobic classrooms of cold brick.

I was frightened by unknown things.
I gradually grew tall.

I became addicted to cigarettes after I gave up toys.

I don't wear short trousers anymore
even though I have nice legs.

I was born in the fifty first autumn of the century.
I now live in a treehouse of my own.

BLUSH

On the morning my feet stop growing
a comet dives
into a shark-infested swimming pool
and a mythological island rises
like a large blind hippopotamus,
with *for sale* signs stuck in its back
like harpoon flags.

On the morning my feet stop growing
I bequeath a Mickey Mouse mug
to archaeological research
and begin compiling an atlas
of ice-cream parlours and beach huts,
a constellation of package tours,
a United Nations of Summer Holidays
with Cliff Richard as the President
and the fifty previous Miss Worlds
huddled together on a stamp.

On the morning my feet stop growing
I decide I don't want a girlfriend
with a mobile phone
or a politically correct
ten out of ten lover.

I want a soul mistress with eccentric feet.

I'm in the library shopping for a wife,
she comes in wearing an egg box
dripping sunny yellow.

On the morning my feet stop growing
a human rights observer mingles
with guests at a shotgun wedding.

When my father married my mother
she went as a snowball.

When I fell for you I melted in brokenness.

On the morning my body attained adulthood
men may have walked on the moon
in the feet of a much larger animal.

On the morning my hands stop growing
my bare feet no longer blush.

GUTHRIE TO GINSBERG

All those old troubadours
who wanted to be folk singers
like Woody Guthrie,

singing songs about
this homeless world,
working the cafés and bars
all along the waterfront.

Six strings and a suitcase
of borrowed mythologies.
Playing the covers
of a previous generation.

One eye on freedom.
One eye on the rainbow.

And all those hobo shoes
who wanted to travel
from one end of the sunset
to the other.

Who closed their doors
every morning
and opened them
again at night,

to sleep in the same
old bed of dreams
like stay-at-home Jack Keroaucs.

Who never went any further
than the railway station
to watch fossilised trains
haul romance and adventure
through a haze of primal smoke.

Frontiersman of a kind.

One eye on the world.
One eye on the table,

And all those blacksmiths
who wanted to be beat poets
like Allen Ginsberg, Gregory Corso,
Lawrence Ferlinghetti,

at a time when I was a young man
and you were a young man,
growing up in sunflower backyards
in the fifties and the sixties
of the twentieth century.

One eye on the girl next door.
One eye on America.

BRUCE DERN

I don't want to be Bruce Dern
any more than necessary.
I want my old name back,
the one my mother gave me
before she moved me and Monica
to Chatsworth Gardens
and Buckingham Shed,
the year Queen Log
was born in Hatfield.
I was watching the Potter's Wheel.
This was before my younger sister
was given a part in the Honicknowle movie,
back in the days when Shirley Temple
grew up on black and white television.

Back in the days when television
was the king of night
and the wireless the king of day
I already had a famous double,
growing up on the small screen streets
of domestic cinema, and no-one knew that,
so I could play whoever I wanted to play,
which was ten times out of nine, a cowboy.
I always wanted to be a baddie and wear
a wild west mask and ride off into the sunset.
I always thought it was cool to leave town
at that time of day on such a slow thing
as a horse. I've always been attracted
to the nebulous and impractical.

I want my old name back, want it reinstated,
I'm camera shy and partial to corners.

I don't want to be famous
for being a tribute actor

or lookalike double.
I don't want to be a superstar's shadow.
Don't want to fall off a second-hand horse,
while riding into the sunset on Sunset Boulevard.

I don't want to go down in dust
as the twin of an American stranger.

I don't want to emigrate to Hollywood
and live inside a cowboy movie.

I'm happy living in the Honicknowle Hills
with my Bob Seger records.

THE SHADOWS OFF THE WALL

I'm listening to The Shadows
playing live at Butlin's,
Bognor Regis, circa
Nineteen Sixty Five.

I'm thinking about Cyrille,
Bognor's younger brother,
who became a professional footballer
and played for West Bromwich Albion,
Coventry City and Aston Villa.

Born between Halloween
and Guy Fawkes night
on the second of November
Nineteen Fifty One,
I share my birthday
with Bruce Welch
and the publisher of
The Honicknowle Book of the Dead.

I can remember yesterday
as if it were years ago.

I'm smooching with Pauline,
a buxom redheaded redcoat
from Harewood Crescent.

The Shadows are playing
'The Honicknowle Green Green Grass
of Home'
on Pauline's Dansette,
followed by 'Apache'
and 'Wonderful Land'.

Across the lino of the dining room floor
Pauline presses against me in stereo.

Downtown at The Tarantula,
Jet Harris is wearing
a brand new pair of winklepickers
and jiving like Harry Webb on mogadon.

Harry Webb is singing
'Little Town Flirt',
a Del Shannon song,
for the under-forty-five nights
down at the Woodland Fort Hippodrome.

I can't afford to take Pauline there
on a paper boy's wages,
so I stay at home and think about
being grown-up and married.

In my bedroom I listen
to 'Geronimo' on the radio.

When Hank Marvin
became a Jehovah's Witness
The Shadows added
'All Along the Watchtower'
to their playlist, and put it on
their mid-seventies long-player
recorded live at the Kingdom Hall
on Crownhill Road.

Hank Marvin and Bruce Welch
were also famous for their stage walk,
which is as everyone knows
as good as choreography gets.

When Bruce and Hank landed
on the Moon in Nineteen Sixty Nine
they became the first air guitarists
in space to play John Cage's
'Four Minutes and Thirty Three Seconds',
four years and thirty three days
before it was written.

Frank Sixsmith and I
once took part in a choral version
of 'Four Minutes and Thirty Three Seconds',
conducted by the composer, Sam Richards.
This version was especially notable
for an encore of sparklers,
and during the intro
Damaris Barber's
percussive uncorking
of a bottle of Bordeaux
is followed by glug glug glug
in perfect time,
which John Cage
would have quietly applauded.

It would have sounded great
on Pauline's Nineteen Fifty Six
Wurlitzer Centennial Jukebox
as a medley with Bruce Welch's Air Gibson
and Hank Marvin's Les Paul.

A Rough Guide to Birdsong

The seven wonders of the world
are the Seven Dwarves
who took a short cut across the seven seas.

The Magnificent Seven and the Seven Samurai
who stayed at home to star in the musical
Fourteen Brides for Fourteen Brothers.

The radio on the sideboard
playing the Temperance Seven
to a bunch of heavy metal moths
headbanging philip's lightbulb.

The Blue Monkey where Darwin drank.

The twenty six blackboards of West Park Infants.

The Honicknowle Reading and Recreation Rooms
built in nineteen twenty seven
the year my father first picked up *Lorna Doone.*

The street sign at the bottom of Chatsworth Gardens
leaning slightly to the left of Woolaton Grove.

Woodland Fort, birthplace of the rocking horse.
There were Apaches living behind it in Woodland Wood
who came around to our house to watch *Boots and Saddles.*

Buckingham Shed, which moves around the lands
of the housing estate and the village,
monitoring street corners, car boot sales, coffee mornings.

The historic Anderson shelters on Tamar Way
which survived the Second World War but not the city council.

Warwick Manor on Butt Park Road,
home to grandfathers and grandmothers.
Warwick Orchard was west of Warwick Manor
and shared a fence with Honicknowle Secondary.
When the secondary and primary schools were demolished
Warwick Orchard's apple trees were cut down
in the gold rush for housing land
to make way for Warwick Orchard Close.
Flocks of homeless birds were taken in by relatives.
Others, conscious of overcrowded family trees
departed on one-way flights to Woodland Wood.
The horses who grazed Warwick Orchard
emigrated to America and became extras on *Lonesome Dove*.

When Honicknowle was listed in the Domesday Book
there were gold-miners impersonating archaeologists
on the banks of Ernesettle Creek
and Vikings lurking in the subconscious.
The New World was hundreds of years away from New York,
and Scott was a figment of the future.

Walking through my home town down the Crownhill Road,
back to the lost world of the motorbike and sidecar,
the box-room and the unexplored wardrobe,
back to Queen Log country
and Woodland Wood Nature Reserve,
where radios in the trees play a rough guide to birdsong.

HEADBANGER

It's your birthday,
you're forty eight and I've forgotten
but you're not fazed.

You take me out and buy me lunch.
We're sat next to each other
in some swanky restaurant,
sharing your personal stereo.
I'm wearing the left earpiece,
you're wearing the right,
everything's equal.

We're listening to Metallica,
their Nineteen Eighty Four record,
a collective protest opposed
to Capital Punishment.

Rock band amplified
against the electric chair.

You've become a headbanger,
an air-guitar player,
you're forty eight,
and you're not fazed.

I like this sharing
and your taste in men.

You're smiling and staring
into my stitched-up eye.

You've been staring into it
for seven years now,
seven years of electricity
and stark naked sunshine.

It's your birthday.
I'm holding your
forty eight year old hand,
you're holding mine,
which is four years older.

We're dining out
on a two-hour honeymoon,
eating lentil this and lentil that.

Last year when I was fifty two
I was halfway through the day
before I remembered
and then only because
you came around
and took me out to lunch
where I was anyway.

It's your birthday,
you're forty eight,
I'm fifty two.

You want a toy boy,
I want a bus pass.

DOGBITE

The corgi that bit me
on Hirmandale Road
must have known
that my dad
didn't like the Queen
as it sunk royalist teeth
into my Republican wrist.

One of the things
my dad used to say,
fairly regular,
was that the Royals
wouldn't invite
the likes of us
around for dinner.

He was right,
they never did.

THE SECOND OF NOVEMBER, NINETEEN FIFTY ONE

Scorpio is my star sign.
Yesterday was my fifty-fifth birthday.
Angie Wickenden proposed
and we were married
and went on honeymoon
to the Crownhill Garden Centre.

I received a birthday card from Nic Ridley,
a birthday card from Susie Shelley,
and a birthday card from Nick Reid,
who I was avoiding because I owed him money.

Angie tells me there are five planets
in Scorpio at the moment.
This is known as a pentangle
and is as close to five a side football
as astrology gets.

Steve Spence once met Danny Thompson.
Danny Thompson once met Steve Spence.
Danny Thompson once played double bass
with the folk group Pentangle.

Steve Spence once sang
angelically in the school choir,
until his voice broke
like a heart might,
or a pirate's bedroom window.

Taurus has been Steve Spence's star sign
since nineteen forty five.

I've no idea what Steve Zodiac's star sign was.

The moon was in Pisces last July in Plymouth,
forty years to the day I first watched *Fireball XL5*.

A television light year or two later,
Stingray swam into our consciousness
through Gerry Anderson's goldfish tank.

Astrologically, Pluto is one of Scorpio's ruling planets.
Now Pluto's planetary status has been decommissioned,
will astronomers (as opposed to astrologers)
be barred from riding on the London Underground?

If today the sun is shining on the European side of the Earth,
will it shine tonight on the American side of the moon?

If I'm the reincarnation of Mercury
where does that leave Postman Pat?

If Neptune is the god of the sea
why has he never been to Plymouth?

DANGERMAN

The donkey that bit my father
on Weston-super-Mare beach
after he'd foolishly stuck
his hand in its mouth,
was called Danny.

Some years earlier a monkey
had done the same thing
when my father offered
it some peanuts
when he slid his hand
into a cage at Bristol Zoo.

He was the kind of man
who'd convince himself
that if he were to place his head
inside the jaws of a Great White Shark
when he pulled it out again
it would still be attached
to his shoulders.

Statistically he wasn't
a very good judge of teeth.

He was the John Drake
of Chatsworth Gardens,
but mostly only a danger to himself.

One Sunday afternoon he was driving
his moped across Dartmoor
when the engine conked out.
He climbed off, opened the tank
and lit a match to see if he'd run
out of petrol.

Stupidity suited him.

He had the kind of faith
that could get you killed.

HAIRNET

My grandmother wore a hairnet like Ena Sharples.
My grandmother looked like Minnie Caldwell
and was a pin-up on my dad's dartboard.

My grandmother had a dog called Bobby
and a goldfish called Steve.
My grandmother drank stout and sang karaoke
in a Rover's Return tribute bar.

My grandmother was born
in Queen Victoria's backyard.
We called her Mrs. Buckingham.
She should have been Albert Tatlock's
live-in-lover, or Leonard Swindley's
post-war bride, before he went off
to command Dad's Army.

She would have made a great Bette Lynch
Annie Walker or Ena Sharples.
She would have looked great
in a platinum blonde wig
with hairnet underneath.

My grandmother's hairnet came from
the gift shop at Granada.
It was a family heirloom.
Sometimes she used it
as a fishing net to catch
the goldfish called Steve,
and even though she wore it
on the day she died of his disease,
my grandmother never met Cecil Parkinson.

WOODLAND WOOD

1

Trees that hang men for murder
give birth to baby crows.

The trees in Woodland Wood have grown
forty years into the sky.

If I'd grown as tall as my carbon dioxide cousins
I'd need a longer raincoat, longer arms,
and a bigger umbrella to keep my skin dry.

When clouds fall like the gravity of love falls
then leafless in rut with Queen Log
I sleep and wake in Woodland Wood.

Under the Abercrombie arches of Whitleigh Bridge I walk
through the young country of childhood with Queen Log
towards the Palmerston architecture of Knowle Fort.
The landscape beneath my wooden stick still springy
with the vigour of youth.

2

I walk into trees in dreams and they turn
into beautiful women.

Walking through the woodland, walking through itself,
soft bodies in New York and London legs
leave the forest for the jungle.

Woodpeckers dig holes in the flesh of beautiful women
and fly inside hotel rooms of soft accommodation.

Beautiful women sway into the small hours
under the healing properties of neon.

On a dance floor slippery with smiles
I sway in the arms of a woman from Orchard Mead,
moving to a slow Hatfield and the North number.

I look into brown eyes and see its almost autumn,
and sense myself falling for slender limbs of sycamore,

and feel the wind move and the earth move
in this bright room of song,

and arrive home from the dance floor to discover
the rocking chair gone and a woman I don't know,
wearing the wedding dress I bought my wife for Christmas.

The rocking chair tells me she's from Woodland Wood,
she's just won the Two Thousand and Two Miss World contest.

WALKING WITH LORNA DOONE

I stare out into space and launch myself
above the landscape of mires
and bright yellow gorse,
and imagine myself to be
a pilot in a quiet aircraft.
Like witchcraft I'm a rook
who's read too much
Carlos Castañeda.

A blue and yellow kite
brightens the landscape,
given freedom of the sky.
The wind as superpower
pulls a young man
across the ground,
levitation or bust.

Looking down dark cul-de-sacs
into hidden valleys,
sweeping one blue eye
over this bleak and beautiful landscape,
I'm reminded of another moorland
as down the backroads of memory
Lorna Doone comes riding,
the most beautiful woman
on my father's bookshelf,
a pin-up for the imagination,
brought to life behind
a quiet pair of reading glasses.

R.D. Blackmore wrote *Lorna Doone*
when Honicknowle was still a country village,
two miles from the edge of Dartmoor,
five miles from the edge of the sea,
south of Woodland Wood,
north of Weston Mill.

Driving out of the city to Dartmoor
on Sunday afternoon
we adjust with ease
from bomb-site to council estate,
from seaside town to bright yellow gorse.

On the King's Highway we cross the River Dart
somewhere between Princetown and Hexworthy
and begin the long climb up snake-twist hills
through Holne and Scoriton without blinking,
past Brook Mill and its live-in peacock
hidden like gold in a rich man's shirt.

Driving from urban wild to country wild
we park between hedgerows
and move onto a moorland track.

Under Ludgate's arch of trees
I imagine the surrealists of Heyford Hall
waving as if we were fish up from the seaside
swimming in formation towards Frog Hall.

Ninety three million miles from the surface of the sun
to a green bungalow and bright yellow gorse
at the end of this sunday afternoon tunnel.

On arrival characters of past life and present life
and fiction merge in the garden and gaze
into the beauty of the tadpole pond
then move like dancers towards the rustle of dry paper
and pirates walking backwards across the sea.

QUEEN LOG

The day moves on, night is pulling it.
I take your hand and we walk
from the Bagatelle to the supermarket,
from the supermarket to the red forty three.
I'm carrying your shopping bags
forty years after carrying your homework home
from school.

The house is dark where we sleep
and our bodies
are passed from one dream to the next
down a long tunnel of cinematic arms.
How gentle these women are
who shelter us,
babysitters from the fall of day
to the rising of brown eyes staring into blue.

The sun shines even at night,
I can see it shining on the moon's empty beaches.

You're singing down the telephone,
the nine lives of love songs
we sing in separation.

Would you miss me
if I was on another landscape?

Moving from the court of Queen Log
I sleepwalk to the living room light switch
in twenty seconds
I'm somewhere on the map of Plymouth,
moving quietly above an alphabet of streets.

The night comes alive,
the language of alcohol spills like an old song,

an a cappella cover.
The age-old echoes of slurred speech
reminds me of the buzz
I'm no longer a part of;
the poetry that is saturday night.

I shuffle in colour coordinated pyjamas,
following the signpost towards the kitchen.

I drop a pyramid teabag into a fifty year old mug
and think about Mister Habib,
who came all the way from Egypt
to stitch my blue eye with silver thread.

Across the courtyard a neighbourhood owl
sits passively at three o'clock in the morning,
socialising with a cop movie.

I can hear the sirens of real life and fiction
on the streets of New York,
on the streets of the twin cities,
on the streets of my hometown, crowded with revellers
who've just awoken me from a conversation
I was having with my girlfriend.
Now she's not talking to me in her sleep.

The house is dark where we sleepwalk.
The house is five miles from my hometown
and two hundred and fifty miles from yours.
Honicknowle twinned with Hatfield.

Tonight the rain falls as I fell
for your brown hair, brown eyes and freckles.

Tonight the Queen of Loneliness isn't your maiden name.

Home Town Nineteen Fifty One

The sea is my home town.
I was born at the mouth
of the River Yealm
on a November afternoon
when the waves were epileptic.

I couldn't speak a word of the language,
but luckily there were people here who could.
I was looking forward to everything
my mother dreamed about inside.

I was born on All Souls' Day.
I don't recall seeing Lobsang Rampa
or Simon Templar.
I looked like a skinny Tibetan buddha
no-one was going to come
all the way to Honicknowle
from the Himalayas to find.
I was crying in my mother's arms,
sailing towards the National Health Service
and the long hill to Freedom Fields.

I was born in November Fifty One
but not Area Fifty One.

The Honicknowle Book of the Dead
was born in nineteen ninety seven
or nineteen ninety eight,
at the mouth of a thought,
while walking to Angie's house
from my home town of the future
to my home town of the past.

Walking through the landscape
of the lands of the dead

I began to imagine
meeting old friends
on street corners,
friends I hung out with
between the age of five and nineteen.

My old childhood friends remained invisible,
although I caught glimpses of them
through the net curtains of memory.

Each time I approached Woodland Fort
or Burrington Secondary
the white noise of the past
began to take on a sense
of audible resolution:

The Honicknowle Book of the Dead,
the history of history and the history of fiction.
Stingray and *Fireball XL5,*
Auntie Maud and *The Man from Uncle,*
The Prisoner and The Great Train Robbery,
my dad smoking Number Six cigarettes
on the platform at Sidmouth Junction,
the Americans sending a rocket to the moon
one month after it passed over our house,
heading for Woodland Wood
and The People's Republic of Whitleigh.

I watched the skies for weeks after that
waiting for people from somewhere else
to land on Chatsworth Gardens
or on the playing fields
that led to Woolaton Grove
and the West Park shops,
but all I saw were small aircraft
flying through the neighbourhood,
looking for the sequel to World War Two.

My father never talked
about the Second World War.
I knew nothing about beaches.
I played cowboys with the dead,
who told goldfish stories.

I once saw sinister looking men
near Crownhill Secondary.
There was an army of them
wearing grey uniforms.

My cousin said they were German soldiers.

Thinking World War Two had made a comeback,
thinking my mother would run with our shadows
through the back door and across the park
to catch a number twelve bus
heading west towards Woodland Fort
and the Blue Monkey, before disappearing
into the St. Budeaux Triangle,
I told her German soldiers
were marching up the street.
She sat there calmly in that
prefabricated shrine to lino,
shuffling memories of blitz city
and told me they weren't German soldiers
but dustmen working for Plymouth City Council.

But memories fade like ink does on so many stories,
and now I look into the faces of strangers
for a trace of recognition,
an acknowledgement of history,
a timeshare of an earlier time,
but all I meet are ghosts
that are not my ghosts.

My ghosts live
in the street corner archives

of the swinging sixties
with Tarzan, Norman Vaughan
and Suzy Creamcheese,

but it's too late in the evening
to travel forty years back in time
to meet them tonight in some post-teenage time-warp.

Instead I pass the quiet shops,
a stranger in my home town;
geographically and emotionally
don't belong anywhere else,
except in the street map of my lover's arms.

If I had three wishes my three wishes
would be to live with you
in a house somewhere in the old village
or on the post-war housing estate
where my family settled,
but it's too late in the evening
to travel into the future
and impossible to quicken time,
so I gaze at Easterbrooks
where I worked as a paper boy
until nineteen sixty seven
then head downhill towards Ramillies Avenue,
approaching an area which forty years ago
would have been considered enemy territory.
Walking to the top of Budshead Road,
en route to Ernesettle,
the streets of the estate
named after World War Two airfields,
passing Ernesettle Primary School,
a hundred feet above sea level,
all the way down Biggin Hill
for a soft landing in the arms of Angie.

THE HOUSE ON HONICKNOWLE LANE

The house is where the birds have come to land and live
from above and beneath the ceiling they sleep and fly.

The house was built for stories to be collected and read.
From cover to undercover, the sperm of archaeology
in the eyes of the architect.

The house is dark. We make movies in our sleep.
The scripts never make sense come the sequel of morning.

The house is five miles from the sea and its gangs of pirates,
who bob about, ship-lift and salvage
with pre Industrial Revolution tools of sword and flintlock.

The bed and the sea bed are twinned with the Earth and the sky.

The house has two bedrooms with brown and blue windows.

At night I walk through the lands of the house,
thinking about an horizon of flesh,
thinking about the coven of the bed.

I'm an owl in the dark my skin is invisible.
This is my tree, in the neighbourhood of others,
my home in the sky, above the bungalows by the river.

Every night inside the house I emigrate to the land of sleep,
to my second home under the duvet. free of the street corner
until morning finds me homesick.

I know my bedtime movies will never be shown
on bedtime television my bedtime stories will never be told,
but who will write down and record the minutes of sleep?

Inside the house, the radio talks to itself, and I talk to myself,
and talk to myself, a language shared with others
not included in this conversation.

Inside the house the television dominates
with twenty four hour small talk.

I'm reading Cormac McCarthy and thinking about eating
a bar of Galaxy from the underground supermarket.

All the pretty lights are galloping across the room.

The cowboy movie is wild
but the television is a domestic appliance.

The house is in orbit around the sun and back,
like walking hand in hand around the block
we rise with the sun for breakfast and set the table for tea.

I take your hand and fall asleep gazing into your brown eyes.

When you're away from home I write love poems
and sleep with them, in the aftermath of your arms.

Late at night I walk through the quiet rooms of the house.
While I'm yours I'll never know love in a bungalow.

Some nights I snore like a foghorn
and mermaids grow feet to reach me.

Tomorrow I may wake to find you crocheting a hat
in the bright colours of a flowerbed I lay
on a quilt in the back garden.

I'm a happily married man.
I've been happily married for two weeks now.
Celebrating the anniversary of a fortnight of bliss.

The house we live in is in the constellation of romance.
The house we live in is on Honicknowle Lane.

I'm in the greenhouse with the bumblebee queen.
We're just come back from our honeymoon
in Buckingham Shed. We're eating dinner
and organising an exhibition of wedding memorabilia.

The future's looking bright for double egg and chips,
but the past never invites you back for lunch.

THE DARK

Who was it that stood in the corner
of the box-bedroom
when I was a small boy
waiting at the bus stop of sleep
to seal the envelope of darkness?
Was it Jesus lifting a glass of red wine
to toast the housing estate we lived on?
Was it a native of my imagination
grown in the vineyards of Chatsworth
or a shadow created by the absence
of electricity?

Was it an independent presence I sensed,
with no umbilical connection to me,
or was it a mechanism created by a marriage
of thought and chemical impulse
to counterbalance homegrown phobias
and monsters who lurk scientifically invisible
above the footstep of every unidentified sound?
lurking stage left of the light
on the dark side of the light-switch.

Whoever or whatever it was, or wasn't,
it never once broke into a sweat
of physical language,
no creak of lips, no tree-like breath
touched my six-year-old ears
or rustled the sleeves of my pyjamas,
never came downstairs for breakfast
bleary-eyed with benevolence,
or inserted a key into a door
between back to back worlds.
It just stood in the corner
like a faithful archetype,
silent as the teddy bear I clutched

until sleep invited me in
to audition for tomorrow.

All around my sleeping body
the house settled and shifted,
distributing weight and wealth,
the day's temperature leaking
from its timbers and sinews like blood;
this Frankenstein of raw materials
culled from forest, mineshaft and quarry.

When night falls on Chatsworth Gardens
and the zodiac is in the constellation of Ford
I'll lay in the box-room dark
tuning into the floorboards noisy feet,
eavesdropping on the conversations of ghosts
in the Honicknowle dead of night
and the creak of the house mumbling to itself
in a tongue older than English.

Cancer

My mother's dead,
she's been dead
for eleven years.

She wasn't a beatnik
or anything like that.

In the last few weeks
of her life
she stopped watching
Coronation Street

and switched channels
to morphine.

MYTHOLOGICAL HONICKNOWLE

Drake, the Elizabethan sea captain,
was married in the same church
as my younger sister.
After the wedding service
he walked with his bride
and their company of pirates
across the Green and through the site
of the unconsecrated Blue Monkey,
kicking the honeymoon off
with a pub-crawl down in the lush
lowlands of Honicknowle,
staggering between the Broomball Arms
and the Buckingham Bierkeller.

My sister and her husband were married
in Higher St. Budeaux Parish Church
in Nineteen Seventy Three.
And now thirty years later
they arrive in a white roller
for a marriage blessing;
the first time any of us
have been back to this medieval church,
overlooking Ernesettle and the River Tamar.

Over four hundred years have passed
as the crow flies backwards,
since Drake walked the lanes
and fields of this district,
through the groves of
Woolaton and Wanstead,
the crescents of Harewood,
Sherford and Shaldon,
the distant avenues of Eastbury,
Byron and Burns,

the gardens of Woodbury,
Shenstone and Chatsworth.

Drake, sixteenth-century golden boy,
frontiersman of the ocean,
set sail from Honicknowle Creek
on a ship made from Woodland Wood oak.
Woodland Wood, where we ran as children,
picking bluebells to plant in water,
bluebells which always grew best outdoors,
bluebells that were gifts for the house
and the birds who lived
in the tallest branches of the house.

Birdsong was a nightly lullaby
until morning broke out of night's eggshell
and we flew like those birds down the stairs,
in search of breakfast,
ravenous after miles of sleep,
gallivanting over dream's playground
where under strange skies and tall trees
troops of monkeys danced
to hidden radios in the air,
cousins to the one who sat
on your shoulder that day
in Tintagel where you could
have been the daughter of Guinevere
or one of the diners at Arthur's table
with a surname like Knight.

One of our mum's twin brothers
was called Arthur. Uncle Arthur
and the Knights of the Round Table
met four times a year,
a mile down the road
from the Blue Monkey,
in the court of Woodland Fort.

Woodland Fort is situated
on the Crownhill Road
with Woodland Wood at its back,
and Honicknowle Green,
a crow's glide away.

Woodland Fort and Camelot
are one and the same.

Avalon is the old name for West Park.

The Holy Grail was a pasty shop.

Merlin's cave was somewhere between
Camel's Head and Camelot.

Camelot is a two-minute
walk from Whitleigh Bridge.

Geoffrey of Monmouth hid Camelot
in mythological Honicknowle.

Excalibur evaporated
from a rain puddle
on the corner of Little Dock Lane
and Ashburnham Road.

SUNDOWN

I get sentimental when the sun goes down
into the river over these hills.

Such a small landscape,
the side of a valley.

This place called Honicknowle,
a map the size of a flannel.

A train runs to the north-east of here,
crosses Ernesettle Creek,
meanders all the way to Calstock.

My mother had friends in Ernesettle;
we'd walk down Biggin Hill
to Tangmere Avenue
right through the middle of the estate
like a family of cowboys,
my mother leading, with no sense
of the dangers small boys faced.

The word in the playground
was that kids who lived in Ernesettle
were at war with kids from Whitleigh.
It was the kind of war
that starts after breakfast,
breaks off for lunch
and is finished in time for tea,
the kind of war you can laugh about
from the distance of adulthood,
but from a small boy's perspective
there were areas to be avoided,
like a doormat best left uncrossed.

Whitleigh is east of Ernesettle,
facing it across a valley
of trees and mudflats,
and north-east of Honicknowle,
with only Woodland Wood
and Whitleigh Bridge
separating the two.

My footsteps hug the past
and I return, heading south
over Whitleigh Bridge,
but there's nothing here but fog.

Honicknowle Secondary is gone
and with it a monument to Abercrombie.
I walk like a lonely architect through this graveyard
and think about the lizards the rocket science
teacher brought back from Italy.
Do they still wander the streets
like refugees from the education system
after the cancellation of biology class?

Like a funeral director with a business card
I walk in a slow circle at sundown
from Woodland Fort to Woodland Fort.

No half-grown ghosts
shout from either playground
or in the street or from the park
behind the houses, where I grew
inch by inch and year by year
before topping out at six foot two.

No echo comes back
from wherever the past is archived.
I could search for a sense of it forever
and not see it pass before me

again and again like Siddhartha
on a loop.

The streets that led off prefabbed Tamar Way
were taken away for burial thirty years ago,
as in other parts of the city,
leaving only a wasteground of neglect.

The prefabs below Chatsworth Gardens
were the homes of explorers.
Shackleton's lawn was white,
the colour of Johnny Winter's hair.
Shackleton played Texas-style blues guitar,
keeping Columbus awake
when the weather was cold.
When the prefabs came down
Shackleton moved further north
and started gigging in Ernesettle
and the People's Republic of Whitleigh.

Honicknowle was discovered
by a distant relative of Scott.
Scott's relative built Chatsworth Farm,
which evolved into Chatsworth Gardens.

I played cowboys with James Coburn
and robbed piggy banks for a living
and started The Honicknowle Blues Band,
the year I read *Nineteen Eighty Four*.

Chatsworth Gardens, where my life began,
is a cul-de-sac of forty houses.
I lived next door to the girl next door
and four down from Patrick McGoohan.

I was a keen mountaineer, climbing
to the box-room above the front garden.

One minute on the peak of the Matterhorn,
the next in the Himalayas with Cyril Henry Hoskins.

That was then and this isn't.

Now I step inside the kitchen onto worn green lino,
and visit each room, walk around the table, set for
dinner or tea, imagine the eight eyes of the past,
brown and blue, open, like doors to the future.
Note the quiet presence of wedding photos.
The Marie Celeste print, gone from the wall.
The reading glasses on the mantelpiece
waiting for Thomas Hardy
or James Fennimore Cooper.

Like a tooth fairy
back in the world of sixpence,

back walking through the lands
and the heart of the house,

listening for the breath of old memories,

but there's no-one home, no sense of being,
as if the people who lived here, including me,
have moved on to other streets, other houses,
other movies, other gardens, other grounds,

racing towards a future
that quickly became wrinkled.

STATE HILL

The official name for this road is Victoria Road,
named to honour a dead queen,
who was born in the previous century
under a walnut throne, hundreds of miles
from the plank palace of Buckingham Shed.

I collected Victoria's worn brown pennies
and thought myself a millionaire
because some of them had been
in and out of pockets
since eighteen thirty seven.
How many rich hands of flesh
have become the X-ray's future?

The locals called Victoria Road, State Hill.
The crown of State Hill was the State Cinema,
a detached building built in the nineteen twenties.
to show silent movies.

When film-makers discovered language
people who went to the cinema learned to talk.
On the slopes of State Hill history parallels fiction.
The history of speech is, in part, the history
of technology.

When humans discovered
how to manipulate the vocal cords,
syllables mated in an alphabet of sound.
Articulating the human tongue put a stop
to the piano becoming the dominant language.

The First World War
was recorded in complete silence.
The mouths of the dying
opened and closed

as if the whole thing
had been dubbed
by tanks of goldfish.
By the time I was born
everyone was talking about
the films of The Second World War.

The blitz was a memory
older Plymothians carried around inside.
I couldn't see through
the brown and the blue
and the broken windows.

The State Cinema looked like a council house.
It was big enough to be a mansion,
a stately home for the working class,
built in an era when men were
not yet dumper-truck drivers
and cranes were not quite herons—
when cheese was cheese and cholesterol
was sneaking around in the dark
and the future was an unsliced sandwich.

When the State Cinema closed,
the cinema shape-shifted into a snooker hall.
In the interests of continuity
night followed day.
Dracula, played by Christopher Lee
wearing a waistcoat, passes the keys
of the building over to Ray Reardon.

As if holding rifles, men with long sticks
look from one end of the stick to the other
the first One Four Seven in St. Budeaux,
recorded live on local radio.

Reaching for the chalk,
reaching for the unreachable sky,
riding multiple shotgun
on a cavalcade
of State Hill stagecoaches
towards Foundation Primary
and The Blue Monkey,
the road bending away
from the symbolic narrative
of a film-set sun set.

After dark Robert Mitchum was a familiar face
in the frontier settlement of Woodland Fort.
When he rode down the trail from Caradon Hill
the streets emptied,
became a glimpse
of the ghost town to come.

When I grow up I want to be a cowboy
and shoot people for a living.
Earn a reputation for being quick on the draw.
Go to Art College and study Fine Art.

I want to become Sheriff of Honicknowle County.
I'll keep the peace and the Wild West
in Buckingham Shed for safekeeping.
I'll drive the Wells Fargo stagecoach
back to the bungalow where
Dale Robertson is living.

I'll organise a cattle drive every year
and move them longhorns from one end
of the Fields to the other.

The cattle drive will be
declared complete
when the sun sets,

when the Fields
are covered with cow shit,

when the coffee and beans
are passed around the campfire,

when the farting begins.

When cows are singing
cow songs out on the grass.

When my father's fallen asleep
with *Lorna Doone* in his lap again.

When my mother's in the Corporation village
of Ambridge dancing with Walter Gabriel

I'll be on the rooftop of the State Cinema
listening to The Rolling Stones on Radio Caroline

while below decks in the fog
of another desert island darkness,
an usherette's torch searches the projection box
for a short cut to Treasure Island,
or supper for two on State Hill.
Sharing a bag of chips
on the way home to make a sequel
to *The Honicknowle Book of the Dead*
with the cowboys of Wild West Park.

WANSTEAD GROVE

And King Arthur is linked
to the Spice Girls

and Queen Log to Woodland Wood.
She's waving to us from the family tree.
She's the queen of sleep and sundown.

And David Icke is linked
to Hereford United
and Coventry City

and Glastonbury
to the Torpoint Ferry

and Tintagel to the roundabout
at the end of Montacute Avenue.

And I'm the reincarnation
of someone
no-one's ever heard of.
Harry Dawson,
the Unknown Pedestrian.

And the Loch Ness Monster
is linked to the cat next door
but only through marriage.

And the yeti is still in the closet
waiting for the paparazzi to go home.

And Hollywood is linked
to everything.

And Honicknowle is the centre
of the universe.

And the four riders
of the apocalypse are riding
in the three fifteen at Kempton.

And the search
for the missing link
has been called off
for the night.

And the St. Budeaux Triangle
is the place to go for Ovaltine
and bed and breakfast.

And the train driver
at the end of the ley line
is linked to a bus conductress
on Wanstead Grove.

Printed in the United Kingdom by
Lightning Source UK Ltd., Milton Keynes
139902UK00001B/15/P